Putting God First

Geary Reid

Acknowledgments

Great thanks must be expressed to the following people:

The heavenly Father, for granting me the wisdom and inspiration to record the information in this book, which I began on November 2, 2021, and completed on November 4, 2021; my family, for their continued encouragement and support regarding various challenges; and several people who have assisted with reviewing and editing the book:

- Rendell F. Harry
- Rev. Kenrick Sandy, BSc. MSc.

To you, the reader: have fun while reading, and grasp and practice what you learn so that this world will become a better place. Many people are depending on your guidance. We all need a shoulder to lean on and a hand to guide us.

Rev. Geary Reid
MBA, FCCA, FAAPM, MPM, CAT

Reid's Learning Institute and Business Consultancy

reidnlearn.com

Amazon: amazon.com/author/gearyreid

Facebook: Reid n Learn

Instagram: Reid n Learn

LinkedIn: Reid's Learning Institute
and Business Consultancy

199 Kuru - Kururu, Soesdyke Linden Highway
Guyana, South America

Table of Contents

Introduction

Every believer will face obstacles as they serve the Lord, and these obstacles may give them many reasons to want to give up serving him. However, if they want to be successful as they serve the Lord, then they must be deliberate about putting God first in their lives. Believers can sometimes let down their guard, but God expects them to always be alert and give him the opportunity to work on their behalf.

As Jesus was teaching the disciples, he taught them many important things. One of these lessons was that if they put God first in their lives, all other things will be added to them. There is evidence of many persons in the Bible and in today's society who have put God first in their lives and become victorious. God wants all believers to follow the same example of putting him first in their lives. The Christian walk is never free from problems, but God will defend his children.

There are times when God will ask his children to do things that seem strange to them, but God often does this in order to prove himself to his children and show that he will bless them. When God asked Abraham to sacrifice his only son, it was a hard request for Abraham, but God had a blessing in store for him. In the case of Hannah, God was willing to change her life because she put him first.

Romans 11:33

33 O the depth of the riches both of the wisdom and knowledge of God! how unsearchable are his judgments, and his ways past finding out!

Can you imagine God sending you to a widow for help? Well, God sent Elijah to a widow for help, and on top of that, Elijah asked her to give him a portion of the meal first and then feed herself and her son thereafter. She obeyed the servant of God, and God blessed her greatly because she put him first.

A king was told that he was going to die. This king did not want to die, but rather to live. The king pleaded his cause before his God, and God gave more years to him. There is no telling of what God can do when persons place him first in their lives.

King Solomon was known as the wisest man of his time. This became possible because Solomon asked God for the tools to lead the people. God loved Solomon's unselfish request and gave him more than he asked for.

Mordecai and Queen Esther had a great battle on their hands to deal with, but they knew that their battle was small in the hands of God. They prayed and fasted, and God blessed the Jews because Mordecai and Esther put him first in their lives. Daniel, Shadrach, Meshach, and Abednego proved their God as they were not going to be subjected to the king's evil request. Their God delivered them, and they were promoted.

It would be difficult for a few loaves and fishes to feed many persons, but Jesus placed those items in the hands of God and many lives were fed. Paul and Silas experienced many challenges as they served God, but their God came through for them because they placed him first in their lives.

1. Seek him first

As parents take care of their children, they expect that their children will grow from toddlers to adolescents to young adults, and then eventually have their own families. When children show signs of growth, their parents are often happy because it frees them from having to do certain simple things for their children.

In a similar way, God expects that believers will grow. He has offered many things for believers to grow, but every believer must make use of the things God has provided so that they will grow from year to year. Too many believers are at the same stage as when they were first saved, but God expects that they will grow as they spend more years serving him.

1.1 Growing your life skills

Every individual, whether saved or unsaved, must develop their life skills. Church leaders are delighted when they see believers progressing. Some of the life skills that believers learn can be very important to help their growth in the body of Christ.

When persons are working, their leaders expect them to show signs of independence. They do not expect to have to tell their employees the same thing over and over again. Independence does not license a person to make whatever decision they like, but each person can think and act for themselves, along with some external support.

1.2 Become dependent upon God

Depending on God is applicable to all believers. No believer is so mature that they do not need God. The more a believer grows in God, the more they need him. Some persons may think that they can become familiar with God and that, being his good friend, they can act independently of him. However, God calls for everyone to seek him and to seek him early. This call is not only applicable to church leaders, but to everyone who is named by the name of Christ.

Many persons believe that they have the ability to take care of their future independently, but in reality, only God can take care of their future. Persons think that it is too much to depend upon God, but they must remember that God owns the universe and he can meet their every need, if they only put him first in every situation.

As Jesus was teaching, he told the disciples not to worry about the future. This statement by caused concern then and still does now, since everyone is trying to provide for tomorrow. But Jesus wants people to learn to seek God first, and the God that they know will provide their needs. Jesus knew that his Father has the ability to help all those who put him first. When a person places their confidence in God, knowing that he has the ability to meet their needs, God loves that approach because they are placing their dependency in him.

Matthew 6:25-34

25 Therefore I say unto you, Take no thought for your life, what ye shall eat, or what ye shall drink; nor yet for your body, what ye shall put on. Is not the life more than meat, and the body than raiment? 26 Behold the fowls of the air: for they sow not, neither do they reap, nor gather into barns; yet your heavenly Father feedeth them. Are ye not much better than they? 27 Which of you by taking thought can add one cubit unto his stature? 28 And why take ye thought for raiment? Consider the lilies of the field, how they grow; they toil not, neither do they spin: 29 And yet I say unto you, That even Solomon in all his glory was not arrayed like one of these. 30 Wherefore, if God so clothe the grass of the field, which today is, and tomorrow is cast into the oven, shall he not much more clothe you, O ye of little faith?

31 Therefore take no thought, saying, What shall we eat? or, What shall we drink? or, Wherewithal shall we be clothed? 32 (For after all these things do the Gentiles seek:) for your heavenly Father knoweth that ye have need of all these things. 33 But seek ye first the kingdom of God, and his righteousness; and all these things shall be added unto you. 34 Take therefore no thought for the morrow: for the morrow shall take thought for the things of itself. Sufficient unto the day is the evil thereof.

Everything that is in the world belongs to God. Therefore, when persons put their trust in God and not in things, then God will provide for them. Jesus asked persons not to take any thought for tomorrow, since tomorrow will take care of itself (Matthew 6:33-34). When persons seek the kingdom of God first, then things will be added to them.

1.3 Reasons for seeking God first

Persons make excuses for why they cannot seek God. However, those individuals should instead find reasons why they should seek God first.

Satan wants to do everything to distract believers from serving God, but God has made it clear that he is a jealous God. He wants to be worshipped, and believers must not put anything before him.

Deuteronomy 4:23-24

23 Take heed unto yourselves, lest ye forget the covenant of the LORD your God, which he made with you, and make you a graven image, or the likeness of any thing, which the LORD thy God hath forbidden thee. 24 For the LORD thy God is a consuming fire, even a jealous God.

Since God was so clear that he does not want his children to serve any other gods, he needs the full attention of every individual. As persons serve him, he will do many things to bless them, because of their love and sacrifice towards him.

Figure 1. Why seek God first?

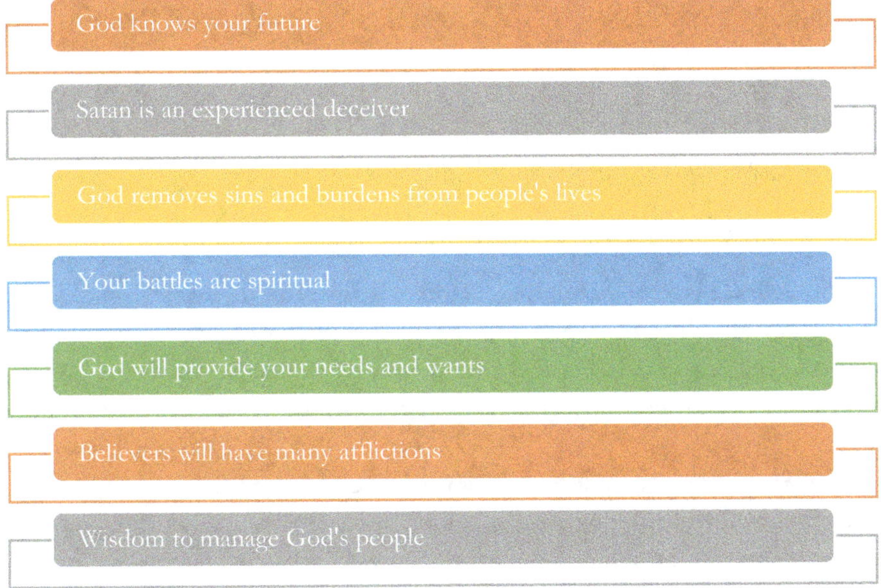

(All figures are developed by the author unless otherwise noted.)

1.3.1 God knows your future

People spend much time trying to find out what their future holds. Some persons will even visit a psychic to enquire about their future. This evil practice often results in persons paying large sums of money for satanic information.

It must be remembered that God created man, and he knows the beginning and the end of every individual. When God made humans, he was certain of what he wanted them to look like and of their purpose on the earth. When God saw the wickedness that his children were practicing, he had a sharp rebuke for them.

Isaiah 46:8-10

8 Remember this, and shew yourselves men: bring it again to mind, O ye transgressors. 9 Remember the former things of old: for I am God, and there is none else; I am God, and there is none like me, 10 Declaring the end from the beginning, and from ancient times the things that are not yet done, saying, My counsel shall stand, and I will do all my pleasure.

Since God knows your future and your end, give him the opportunity to lead you in the future. As you trust God to lead your life, there will be obstacles, but God knows how to navigate you through the storms that will come your way. All of these obstacles are greater than you can handle, but God knows how to enable you to walk through these obstacles and remain standing.

Isaiah 43:2

2 When thou passest through the waters, I will be with thee; and through the rivers, they shall not overflow thee: when thou walkest through the fire, thou shalt not be burned; neither shall the flame kindle upon thee.

1.3.2 Satan is an experienced deceiver

No believer is good enough to compete against the adversary in their own strength. The evil plans of Satan were not concocted only recently. Satan has studied each individual in order to think of ways to make them sin. If he fails in one attempt to get believers to do the wrong things, then he will try another way.

It is Satan's nature to deceive believers. Therefore, he and his demons can spend much time analyzing each individual and presenting them with cunning situations to cause them to fall into the trap of sin.

After God had placed Adam and Eve in the garden, Satan made himself known to them, and he presented one of his traps to them. He shared with them enticing words that were not consistent with God's truth. He wanted to make them sin, and he was successful in his plan.

Take a careful read of the conversation between Satan and Eve in Genesis 3:1-6. Satan, as an experienced deceiver, did not present a challenge to them that would look very difficult. He knew that if it seemed difficult, they might have not tried it and may have seen his sinister plan. He used something simple, and he communicated with Eve because he knew that she was weaker and might be more open to his discussion. Adam was occupied doing the work of the Lord and Eve had some time at her disposal, so Satan had time to engage her in a conversation and to convince her to do something that was seemingly simple but went against the command of God.

Genesis 3:1-14

¹Now the serpent was more subtil than any beast of the field which the LORD God had made. And he said unto the woman, Yea, hath God said, Ye shall not eat of every tree of the garden? ²And the woman said unto the serpent, We may eat of the fruit of the trees of the garden: ³But of the fruit of the tree which is in the midst of the garden, God hath said, Ye shall not eat of it, neither shall ye touch it, lest ye die. ⁴And the serpent said unto the woman, Ye shall not surely die: ⁵For God doth know that in the day ye eat thereof, then your eyes shall be opened, and ye shall be as gods, knowing good and evil. ⁶And when the woman saw that the tree was good for food, and that it was pleasant to the eyes, and a tree to be desired to make one wise, she took of the fruit thereof, and did eat, and gave also unto her husband with her; and he did eat. ⁷And the eyes of them both were opened, and they knew that they were naked; and they sewed fig leaves together, and made themselves aprons.

⁸And they heard the voice of the LORD God walking in the garden in the cool of the day: and Adam and his wife hid themselves from the presence of the LORD God amongst the trees of the garden. ⁹And the LORD God called unto Adam, and said unto him, Where art thou? ¹⁰And he said, I heard thy voice in the garden, and I was afraid, because I was naked; and I hid myself. ¹¹And he said, Who told thee that thou wast naked? Hast thou eaten of the tree, whereof I commanded thee that thou shouldest not eat? ¹²And the man said, The woman whom thou gavest to be with me, she gave me of the tree, and I did eat. ¹³And the LORD God said unto the woman, What is this that thou hast done? And the woman said, The serpent beguiled me, and I did eat. ¹⁴And the LORD God said unto the serpent, Because thou hast done this, thou art cursed above all cattle, and above every beast of the field; upon thy belly shalt thou go, and dust shalt thou eat all the days of thy life.

Satan was rejoicing because he got Adam and Eve to fall to his plan, so he thought he could also try a trick on Jesus to make him fall to his crafty plan too. Satan tried just once and was able to convince Adam and Eve to do the wrong thing, so they fell to his trap. He tried three times to get Jesus to fall into his trap, but Jesus was able to see through his hidden agenda.

The very first verse in Matthew 4 provides a background of why Jesus was led into the wilderness. It is clear that Jesus was not going into the wilderness for a vacation, but he was entering a battlefield. The battle that Jesus had to encounter was not with humans, but with Satan. For Jesus to win this battle, he could not operate in the same way as Adam and Eve did, where they relied on their natural ability to converse with an experienced deceiver.

A comparison to note about Eve and Jesus is that they both spoke to this experienced deceiver. In both cases, Satan approached them first and made a statement that sounded enticing. They both had to respond to him, but what they said and how they made their statements is very important. Eve's response was accommodating to the serpent (Genesis 3:2-6), while Jesus' response was from the uncompromising word of God (Matthew 4:3-9).

Matthew 4:1-11

1 Then was Jesus led up of the Spirit into the wilderness to be tempted of the devil. 2 And when he had fasted forty days and forty nights, he was afterward an hungred.

3 And when the tempter came to him, he said, If thou be the Son of God, command that these stones be made bread. 4 But he answered and said, It is written, Man shall not live by bread alone, but by every word that proceedeth out of the mouth of God.

5 Then the devil taketh him up into the holy city, and setteth him on a pinnacle of the temple, 6 And saith unto him, If thou be the Son of God, cast thyself down: for it is written, He shall give his angels charge concerning thee: and in their hands they shall bear thee up, lest at any time thou dash thy foot against a stone. 7 Jesus said unto him, It is written again, Thou shalt not tempt the Lord thy God.

8 Again, the devil taketh him up into an exceeding high mountain, and sheweth him all the kingdoms of the world, and the glory of them; 9 And saith unto him, All these things will I give thee, if thou wilt fall down and worship me. 10 Then saith Jesus unto him, Get thee hence, Satan: for it is written, Thou shalt worship the Lord thy God, and him only shalt thou serve. 11 Then the devil leaveth him, and, behold, angels came and ministered unto him.

If Satan was able to approach Jesus and tempt him with things that were important to him, then Satan will do the same thing to any other believer. The things Satan suggested to Jesus were not impossible, but Jesus knew Satan's evil intention provided responses that did not give Satan success.

As an experienced deceiver, after Jesus provided a response to one of Satan's suggestions, Satan already had another suggestion for Jesus. It is clear that Satan came well prepared to tempt the Son of Man and he was not willing to give up easily.

Satan is a predator who does not plan to walk away without his victim, so he will keep trying all his possible options to deceive his prey.

The Apostle Peter provided a description of Satan so that believers will know who they have to combat with. Satan is always on a mission to deceive persons.

1 Peter 5:8

8 Be sober, be vigilant; because your adversary the devil, as a roaring lion, walketh about, seeking whom he may devour.

Satan is so cunning, he will appear in different images. Sometimes, he may present himself as an angel of light. Therefore, believers have to combat an enemy who changes his image, personality, and actions.

2 Corinthians 11:14

14 And no marvel; for Satan himself is transformed into an angel of light.

1.3.3 God removes sins and burdens from people's lives

Every human who does not know the Lord is walking around with burdens that they cannot remove from their own lives. These humans are carrying extra weights. However, when these same humans acknowledge the Lord as their help and put him first in their lives, he is able to remove their burden and give them freedom. There is no other option than choosing the Lord to remove the burdens from people's life.

Matthew 11:28-30

28 Come unto me, all ye that labor and are heavy laden, and I will give you rest. 29 Take my yoke upon you, and learn of me; for I am meek and lowly in heart: and ye shall find rest unto your souls. 30 For my yoke is easy, and my burden is light.

Christ wants to set everyone free. His plan for their freedom is not only for today, but freedom forever.

John 8:32, 36

32 And ye shall know the truth, and the truth shall make you free.
36 If the Son therefore shall make you free, ye shall be free indeed.

1.3.4 Your battles are spiritual

Many persons will learn martial arts, judo, or kickboxing because they want to defend themselves. However, those skills can only provide physical protection, and the battles that believers have to fight are not physical battles. Therefore, they cannot prepare themselves to fight these battles in the flesh, but in the spirit. Anyone who is willing to let God fight their spiritual battle must put God first in their lives.

The letter from Apostle Paul to the Ephesians provides all believers with guidance that they are in a spiritual battle and must be well prepared. His letter instructs believers to put on the whole armor of God and not only part of the armor, since believers are not going to war to lose.

Ephesians 6:10-18

10 Finally, my brethren, be strong in the Lord, and in the power of his might. 11 Put on the whole armour of God, that ye may be able to stand against the wiles of the devil. 12 For we wrestle not against flesh and blood, but against principalities, against powers, against the rulers of the darkness of this world, against spiritual wickedness in high places. 13 Wherefore take unto you the whole armour of God, that ye may be able to withstand in the evil day and having done all, to stand. 14 Stand therefore, having your loins girt about with truth, and having on the breastplate of righteousness; 15 And your feet shod with the preparation of the gospel of peace; 16 Above all, taking the shield of faith, wherewith ye shall be able to quench all the fiery darts of the wicked. 17 And take the helmet of salvation, and the sword of the Spirit, which is the word of God: 18 Praying always with all prayer and supplication in the Spirit, and watching thereunto with all perseverance and supplication for all saints.

No believer should entangle themselves in wresting against another believer. They must prepare themselves to wrestle against the adversary and to win their battle against Satan.

Figure 2. With whom are believers wrestling (Ephesians 6:12)?

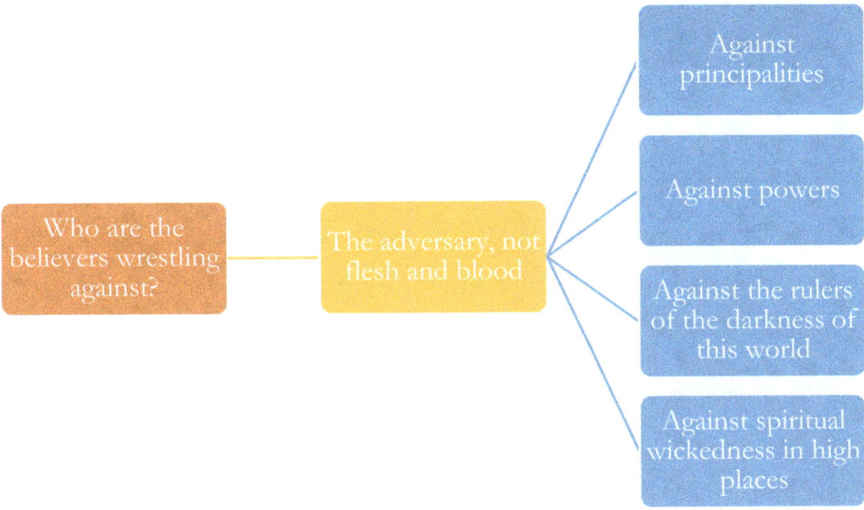

1.3.5 God will provide your needs and wants

As a loving father, God knows that it is his responsibility to provide the needs and desires of his children, and he will do so. Believers must make their request known unto God by asking him, seeking him, and knocking to get his attention.

Psalm 37:4

⁴ Delight thyself also in the Lord: and he shall give thee the desires of thine heart.

Matthew 7:7-8

⁷ Ask, and it shall be given you; seek, and ye shall find; knock, and it shall be opened unto you: ⁸ For every one that asketh receiveth; and he that seeketh findeth; and to him that knocketh it shall be opened.

Believers' needs will be met when they find God. Therefore, they must seek their God first.

John 15:7

⁷ If ye abide in me, and my words abide in you, ye shall ask what ye will, and it shall be done unto you.

Figure 3. Believers' needs are met whenever they find God

Psalm 145:15-19

15 The eyes of all wait upon thee; and thou givest them their meat in due season. 16 Thou openest thine hand, and satisfies the desire of every living thing. 17 The LORD is righteous in all his ways and holy in all his works. 18 The LORD is nigh unto all them that call upon him, to all that call upon him in truth. 19 He will fulfil the desire of them that fear him: he also will hear their cry, and will save them.

As a shepherd, the Lord knows where to lead his flock. He wants his flock to follow him, as he will lead them in paths where their needs and desires will be met.

Psalm 23:1-2, 6

1 The LORD is my shepherd; I shall not want. 2 He maketh me to lie down in green pastures: he leadeth me beside the still waters.
6 Surely goodness and mercy shall follow me all the days of my life: and I will dwell in the house of the LORD for ever.

1.3.6 Believers will have many afflictions

When a person gives their life to the Lord, they must know that it is not an easy journey. Many persons have testified that soon after they made a decision to serve the Lord, many negative things started to affect them.

However, believers have hope that despite their afflictions, God will deliver them if they seek his help.

Believers sometimes believe that they must go through their struggles alone, but if they place God first, they will overcome those struggles. While the struggles are many, God will be there to help every believer, whether they were recently saved or have been saved for many decades.

Believers must praise the Lord before the storm, through the storm, and even when the storm is over. Since believers know that they will have many storms and that God will deliver them, they must remain committed to God and watch and see how he will bring them through their storm.

Psalm 34:1, 15, 19

1 I will bless the LORD at all times: his praise shall continually be in my mouth.
15 The eyes of the LORD are upon the righteous, and his ears are open unto their cry.
19 Many are the afflictions of the righteous: but the LORD delivereth him out of them all.

1.3.7 Wisdom to manage God's people

As believers continue to grow, they may be given the opportunity to manage others. If a believer wants to be an effective leader, then they need to depend upon God to guide them. Believers must not be afraid to ask God for knowledge and wisdom to manage his people.

The approaches used to manage unbelievers will not always be applicable for managing believers. When Solomon was given the opportunity to rule over the children of Israel, he asked God for knowledge and wisdom. He needed these two resources because human learning will always be limited as it relates to leading believers, since the guidance believers need includes both physical and spiritual guidance.

2 Chronicles 1:7-12

7 In that night did God appear unto Solomon, and said unto him, Ask what I shall give thee. 8 And Solomon said unto God, Thou hast shewed great mercy unto David my father, and hast made me to reign in his stead. 9 Now, O LORD God, let thy promise unto David my father be established: for thou hast made me king over a people like the dust of the earth in multitude. 10 Give me now wisdom and knowledge, that I may go out and come in before this people: for who can judge this thy people, that is so great? 11 And God said to Solomon, Because this was in thine heart, and thou hast not asked riches, wealth, or honour, nor the life of thine enemies, neither yet hast asked long life; but hast asked wisdom and knowledge for thyself, that thou mayest judge my people, over whom I have made thee king: 12 Wisdom and knowledge is granted unto thee; and I will give thee riches, and wealth, and honour, such as none of the kings have had that have been before thee, neither shall there any after thee have the like.

1.4 How to seek God first in your Christian journey

The question of how to seek God first is critical for believers. However, God wants believers to utilize the options available to them to seek him.

Figure 4. How to seek God first in your life

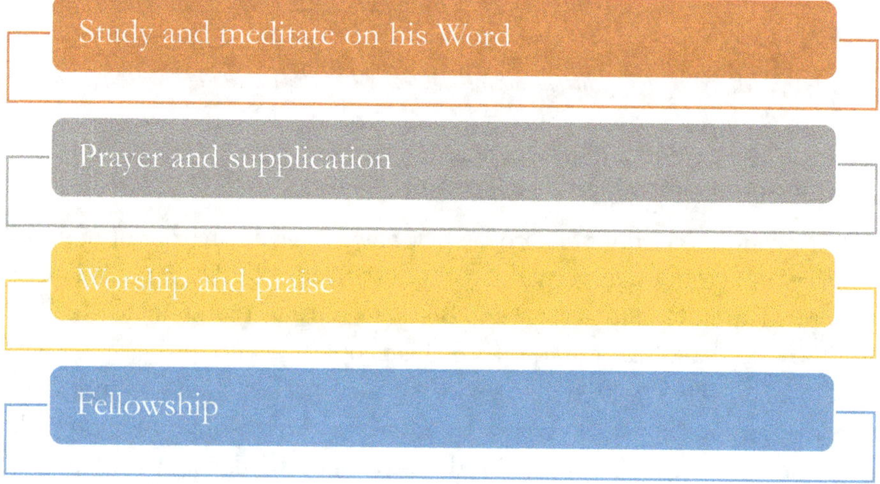

1.4.1 Study and meditate on his Word

When believers go through difficulties, what do they do, and whom should they turn to? The Word of God is a good defense for all believers, and believers are reminded to keep God's words very close to them.

Psalm 119:11

11 Thy word have I hid in mine heart, that I might not sin against thee.

The Word of God must not be treated as an ornament, as it is a living tool that must be put to use daily.

2 Timothy 2:15

15 Study to shew thyself approved unto God, a workman that needeth not to be ashamed, rightly dividing the word of truth.

There are many things that can distract believers and cause their faith to be weakened. Therefore, constantly studying and using of God's Word is good for all believers to do.

Proverbs 7:2-3

2 Keep my commandments, and live; and my law as the apple of thine eye. 3 Bind them upon thy fingers, write them upon the table of thine heart.

God had an early conversation with Joshua, as Joshua had taken over the leadership of Israel after Moses' earthly journey with God had ended. God told Joshua to meditate on the Word and not to let it depart from his mouth. Once Joshua was able to put God's word first in his life, then he was sure to have success.

Joshua 1:8

8 This book of the law shall not depart out of thy mouth; but thou shalt meditate therein day and night, that thou mayest observe to do according to all that is written therein: for then thou shalt make thy way prosperous, and then thou shalt have good success.

When believers study God's Word and apply it to their lives, they will prosper. The success and prosperity of believers is not based on their knowledge, but on their application of God's Word to their lives.

1.4.2 Prayer and supplication

Believers are called to a life of prayer. There are times when believers may not feel like praying and meditating, but they cannot live their Christian life without seeking the presence and power of God.

Philippians 4:6-8

6 Be careful for nothing; but in every thing by prayer and supplication with thanksgiving let your requests be made known unto God. 7 And the peace of God, which passeth all understanding, shall keep your hearts and minds through Christ Jesus. 8 Finally, brethren, whatsoever things are true, whatsoever things are honest, whatsoever things are just, whatsoever things are pure, whatsoever things are lovely, whatsoever things are of good report; if there be any virtue, and if there be any praise, think on these things.

Prayer is not a one-off event. It must be done constantly unto God, and as believers do this, they will see the hands of God working on their behalf. Believers are expected to do those things which are correct in the eyes of the Lord.

1 Thessalonians 5:16-18

16 Rejoice evermore. 17 Pray without ceasing. 18 In every thing give thanks: for this is the will of God in Christ Jesus concerning you.

1.4.3 Worship and praise

God loves worship. He wants his children to worship him daily.

Psalm 34:1-4

1 I will bless the LORD at all times: his praise shall continually be in my mouth. 2 My soul shall make her boast in the LORD: the humble shall hear thereof, and be glad. 3 O magnify the LORD with me, and let us exalt his name together. 4 I sought the LORD, and he heard me, and delivered me from all my fears.

When God is sought, he will deliver believers from the things that they are going through. Believers must pray and praise, since they know that God has the ability to deliver them.

Psalm 63:1-7

1 O God, thou art my God; early will I seek thee: my soul thirsteth for thee, my flesh longeth for thee in a dry and thirsty land, where no water is; 2 To see thy power and thy glory, so as I have seen thee in the sanctuary. 3 Because thy lovingkindness is better than life, my lips shall praise thee. 4 Thus will I bless thee while I live: I will lift up my hands in thy name. 5 My soul shall be satisfied as with marrow and fatness; and my mouth shall praise thee with joyful lips: 6 When I remember thee upon my bed, and meditate on thee in the night watches. 7 Because thou hast been my help, therefore in the shadow of thy wings will I rejoice.

1.4.4 Fellowship

Every believer must remember to serve God and love people. Remember that Jesus died for sinners. Therefore, as believers, you must extend the love of God to all persons and let them feel his love through your life.

As Apostle John wrote his epistle, he dedicated much attention towards love, according to 1 John 4:7-21. He wants every believer not merely to talk about love, but to live in love. He reminds believers that they must love people not because of their outward appearance, but because they are God's creation.

1 John 4:7-21

7 Beloved, let us love one another: for love is of God; and every one that loveth is born of God, and knoweth God. 8 He that loveth not knoweth not God; for God is love. 9 In this was manifested the love of God toward us, because that God sent his only begotten Son into the world, that we might live through him. 10 Herein is love, not that we loved God, but that he loved us, and sent his Son to be the propitiation for our sins. 11 Beloved, if God so loved us, we ought also to love one another.

12 No man hath seen God at any time. If we love one another, God dwelleth in us, and his love is perfected in us. 13 Hereby know we that we dwell in him, and he in us, because he hath given us of his Spirit. 14 And we have seen and do testify that the Father sent the Son to be the Saviour of the world. 15 Whosoever shall confess that Jesus is the Son of God, God dwelleth in him, and he in God. 16 And we have known and believed the love that God hath to us. God is love; and he that dwelleth in love dwelleth in God, and God in him.

17 Herein is our love made perfect, that we may have boldness in the day of judgment: because as he is, so are we in this world. 18 There is no fear in love; but perfect love casteth out fear: because fear hath torment. He that feareth is not made perfect in love. 19 We love him, because he first loved us. 20 If a man say, I love God, and hateth his brother, he is a liar: for he that loveth not his brother whom he hath seen, how can he love God whom he hath not seen? 21 And this commandment have we from him, That he who loveth God love his brother also.

When believers demonstrate the love of God towards people, they are giving God an opportunity to work through their lives. God is looking for more believers to demonstrate his love every day of their lives as they help the poor and needy.

2. Abraham put God first

God told Abraham to make a sacrifice, and Abraham was willing to follow God's instructions. What still remains strange to many persons today is that God asked Abraham to use his only son as the sacrifice. This would be a very difficult request for any parent, but Abraham was willing to follow God's instruction and sacrifice his only son. Take note, Isaac was Abraham's only son. However unreasonable it may be for Abraham, God wanted Abraham to put him first.

The journey Abraham had to traverse was long and mountainous, but Abraham was willing to put God first. Abraham's son, Isaac, was willing to obey his father; and as they were on their way to the destination, he asked his father about the lamb, and Abraham provided a response.

Abraham had at least three days to think about the request that God asked of him, but he obeyed God. Abraham had the opportunity to turn back from the journey, but he still obeyed God. Abraham was one man who was willing to put God first.

Genesis 22:1-14

1 And it came to pass after these things, that God did tempt Abraham, and said unto him, Abraham: and he said, Behold, here I am. 2 And he said, Take now thy son, thine only son Isaac, whom thou lovest, and get thee into the land of Moriah; and offer him there for a burnt offering upon one of the mountains which I will tell thee of. 3 And Abraham rose up early in the morning, and saddled his ass, and took two of his young men with him, and Isaac his son, and clave the wood for the burnt offering, and rose up, and went unto the place of which God had told him. 4 Then on the third day Abraham lifted up his eyes, and saw the place afar off. 5 And Abraham said unto his young men, Abide ye here with the ass; and I and the lad will go yonder and worship, and come again to you. 6 And Abraham took the wood of the burnt offering, and laid it upon Isaac his son; and he took the fire in his hand, and a knife; and they went both of them together.

7 And Isaac spake unto Abraham his father, and said, My father: and he said, Here am I, my son. And he said, Behold the fire and the wood: but where is the lamb for a burnt offering? 8 And Abraham said, My son, God will provide himself a lamb for a burnt offering: so they went both of them together. 9 And they came to the place which God had told him of; and Abraham built an altar there, and laid the wood in order, and bound Isaac his son, and laid him on the altar upon the wood. 10 And Abraham stretched forth his hand, and took the knife to slay his son.

11 And the angel of the LORD called unto him out of heaven, and said, Abraham, Abraham: and he said, Here am I. 12 And he said, Lay not thine hand upon the lad, neither do thou any thing unto him: for now I know that thou fearest God, seeing thou hast not withheld thy son, thine only son from me. 13 And Abraham lifted up his eyes, and looked, and behold behind him a ram caught in a thicket by his horns: and Abraham went and took the ram, and offered him up for a burnt offering in the stead of his son. 14 And Abraham called the name of that place Jehovahjireh: as it is said to this day, In the mount of the LORD it shall be seen.

2.1 God blessed Abraham for his obedience

Abraham was faithful to God's request. When he was about to sacrifice his son, an angel of the Lord spoke to him. God blessed Abraham, and that blessing flowed from generation to generation because Abraham obeyed God.

Genesis 22:15-19

15 And the angel of the LORD called unto Abraham out of heaven the second time, 16 And said, By myself have I sworn, saith the LORD, for because thou hast done this thing, and hast not withheld thy son, thine only son: 17 That in blessing I will bless thee, and in multiplying I will multiply thy seed as the stars of the heaven, and as the sand which is upon the sea shore; and thy seed shall possess the gate of his enemies; 18 And in thy seed shall all the nations of the earth be blessed; because thou hast obeyed my voice. 19 So Abraham returned unto his young men, and they rose up and went together to Beersheba; and Abraham dwelt at Beersheba.

God allowed for the sacrifice to continue, but he replaced Isaac with a lamb. This became possible because Abraham was willing to put God first in his life.

3. Hannah put God first

The life of Hannah is a testimony to all believers. She was barren. Her barrenness was not because any wrongdoing; rather, it was God who had shut up her womb. This barren woman could have accepted God's position for her, but she chose to put God first. She poured her heart out to God through prayer.

God could have maintained his position that she would remain barren, but he was about to put a stop to her barrenness. She did not go around the place complaining about her situation; she knew the God whom she served, and she knew that he is a deliverer. Hannah was willing to prove that God would come through for her after she prayed.

1 Samuel 1:9-21

⁹So Hannah rose up after they had eaten in Shiloh, and after they had drunk. Now Eli the priest sat upon a seat by a post of the temple of the LORD. ¹⁰And she was in bitterness of soul, and prayed unto the LORD, and wept sore. ¹¹And she vowed a vow, and said, O LORD of hosts, if thou wilt indeed look on the affliction of thine handmaid, and remember me, and not forget thine handmaid, but wilt give unto thine handmaid a man child, then I will give him unto the LORD all the days of his life, and there shall no razor come upon his head. ¹²And it came to pass, as she continued praying before the LORD, that Eli marked her mouth. ¹³Now Hannah, she spake in her heart; only her lips moved, but her voice was not heard: therefore Eli thought she had been drunken. ¹⁴And Eli said unto her, How long wilt thou be drunken? put away thy wine from thee. ¹⁵And Hannah answered and said, No, my lord, I am a woman of a sorrowful spirit: I have drunk neither wine nor strong drink, but have poured out my soul before the LORD. ¹⁶Count not thine handmaid for a daughter of Belial: for out of the abundance of my complaint and grief have I spoken hitherto. ¹⁷Then Eli answered and said, Go in peace: and the God of Israel grant thee thy petition that thou hast asked of him. ¹⁸And she said, Let thine handmaid find grace in thy sight. So the woman went her way, and did eat, and her countenance was no more sad.

¹⁹ And they rose up in the morning early, and worshipped before the LORD, and returned, and came to their house to Ramah: and Elkanah knew Hannah his wife; and the LORD remembered her. ²⁰ Wherefore it came to pass, when the time was come about after Hannah had conceived, that she bare a son, and called his name Samuel, saying, Because I have asked him of the LORD. ²¹ And the man Elkanah, and all his house, went up to offer unto the LORD the yearly sacrifice, and his vow.

Hannah became pregnant and gave birth to Samuel, and this very Samuel became the first prophet. Hannah's answered prayer was proof that her God heard her prayer. What a great difference it made for Hannah to put God first in her situation. She was willing to commit towards prayer, and God heard her prayer. She did not pray for a child so that she could manipulate the child to do whatever she wanted; she vowed to give her son unto the Lord. God saw her heart and granted her request. Hannah then honored her vow and gave her son unto the works of the Lord.

Putting God first can change barrenness to fruitfulness. Do not quit praying, but stay with God until there is a victory.

4. The widow at Zarephath put God first

No one can predict how God will work. There was a widow at Zarephath, and she was about to eat her last meal and die. Her financial resources had dried up, and she probably had no other support. Strangely, God sent Prophet Elijah to go to her and ask assistance from her. Some persons may see this as an uncaring move from God. However, when God wants to bless someone, he will do many things that people cannot fathom.

In the scripture 1 Kings 17:7-16, God wanted this widow to put him first, and then he was going to bless her. Some persons would expect that God would bless her first and then make a request of her. However, God had a different formula for her, as he wanted her to be a blessing to his servant first, and then he was going to bless her.

1 Kings 17:7-13

7 And it came to pass after a while, that the brook dried up, because there had been no rain in the land. 8 And the word of the LORD came unto him, saying, 9 Arise, get thee to Zarephath, which belongeth to Zidon, and dwell there: behold, I have commanded a widow woman there to sustain thee. 10 So he arose and went to Zarephath. And when he came to the gate of the city, behold, the widow woman was there gathering of sticks: and he called to her, and said, Fetch me, I pray thee, a little water in a vessel, that I may drink. 11 And as she was going to fetch it, he called to her, and said, Bring me, I pray thee, a morsel of bread in thine hand. 12 And she said, As the LORD thy God liveth, I have not a cake, but an handful of meal in a barrel, and a little oil in a cruse: and, behold, I am gathering two sticks, that I may go in and dress it for me and my son, that we may eat it, and die. 13 And Elijah said unto her, Fear not; go and do as thou hast said: but make me thereof a little cake first, and bring it unto me, and after make for thee and for thy son.

4.1 Difficulties experienced by the widow at Zarephath

This widow was already experiencing much difficulty, and then Elijah came along and added more challenges to her. Nevertheless, she was willing to obey the word of the servant of God and place God first above all of her situations.

Figure 5. Difficulties the widow experienced

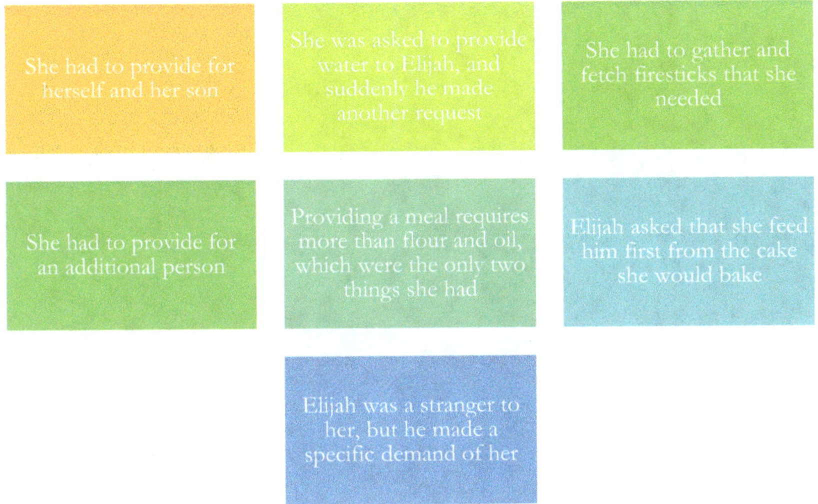

4.2 God blessed the widow at Zarephath after she obeyed Elijah

If Elijah did not visit this widow, then she was indeed going to prepare her last meal, feed herself and her son, and then die. However, God wanted to work a miracle through her and asked her to put him first. She was obedient to God and followed the request of God's servant. In return, God had a blessing for her, and her life was better after she did what God asked her to do.

> *1 Kings 17:14-16*
>
> *14 For thus saith the LORD God of Israel, The barrel of meal shall not waste, neither shall the cruse of oil fail, until the day that the LORD sendeth rain upon the earth. 15 And she went and did according to the saying of Elijah: and she, and he, and her house, did eat many days. 16 And the barrel of meal wasted not,*

neither did the cruse of oil fail, according to the word of the LORD, which he spake by Elijah.

5. Hezekiah put God first

King Hezekiah was sick. No one likes to be sick, and King Hezekiah wanted to continue his reign as a king, so he wanted his life to be spared.

God sent his word through his servant, Prophet Isaiah, notifying King Hezekiah that he was going to die soon. The king was troubled by the statement from the prophet, and he chose to make his problem a matter of prayer.

Whenever persons are troubled, they must take their concern to the Lord. King Hezekiah reminded God of their relationship. God listened to King Hezekiah and was willing to make a change, which caused King Hezekiah to have fifteen years added to his life.

2 Kings 20:1-11

1 In those days was Hezekiah sick unto death. And the prophet Isaiah the son of Amoz came to him, and said unto him, Thus saith the LORD, Set thine house in order; for thou shalt die, and not live. 2 Then he turned his face to the wall, and prayed unto the LORD, saying, 3 I beseech thee, O LORD, remember now how I have walked before thee in truth and with a perfect heart, and have done that which is good in thy sight. And Hezekiah wept sore. 4 And it came to pass, afore Isaiah was gone out into the middle court, that the word of the LORD came to him, saying, 5 Turn again, and tell Hezekiah the captain of my people, Thus saith the LORD, the God of David thy father, I have heard thy prayer, I have seen thy tears: behold, I will heal thee: on the third day thou shalt go up unto the house of the LORD. 6 And I will add unto thy days fifteen years; and I will deliver thee and this city out of the hand of the king of Assyria; and I will defend this city for mine own sake, and for my servant David's sake.

7 And Isaiah said, Take a lump of figs. And they took and laid it on the boil, and he recovered. 8 And Hezekiah said unto Isaiah, What shall be the sign that the LORD will heal me, and that I shall go up into the house of the LORD the third day? 9 And Isaiah said, This sign shalt thou have of the LORD, that the LORD will do the thing that he hath spoken: shall the shadow go forward ten degrees, or go back ten degrees? **10** *And Hezekiah answered, It is a light thing for the shadow to go down ten degrees: nay, but let the shadow return backward ten degrees.* **11** *And Isaiah the prophet cried unto the* LORD: *and he brought the shadow ten degrees backward, by which it had gone down in the dial of Ahaz.*

God is willing to work on the behalf of his children, if they will only put him first. No one ever knows what the outcome will be concerning their prayer, but they must rest assured that God can work in their favor, since he is a loving God and does not want to see his children struggle.

6. Solomon put God first

Once David's reign was over, Solomon was in charge of leading God's people. God was working through the life of Solomon.

Solomon knew that leading people is not always easy. He did not quit on his assignment to lead God's people, but he did need some important resources from God.

When persons ask God for resources to help them to do the work of the Lord, it is often seen that God helps them. While Solomon could have depended on his own wisdom or the wisdom of others to lead God's people, he chose to ask God for God's wisdom to lead his people. Solomon's approach allowed God to bless him with the resources to lead the people of God.

2 Chronicles 1:7-12

7 In that night did God appear unto Solomon, and said unto him, Ask what I shall give thee. 8 And Solomon said unto God, Thou hast shewed great mercy unto David my father, and hast made me to reign in his stead. 9 Now, O LORD God, let thy promise unto David my father be established: for thou hast made me king over a people like the dust of the earth in multitude. 10 Give me now wisdom and knowledge, that I may go out and come in before this people: for who can judge this thy people, that is so great? 11 And God said to Solomon, Because this was in thine heart, and thou hast not asked riches, wealth, or honour, nor the life of thine enemies, neither yet hast asked long life; but hast asked wisdom and knowledge for thyself, that thou mayest judge my people, over whom I have made thee king: 12 Wisdom and knowledge is granted unto thee; and I will give thee riches, and wealth, and honour, such as none of the kings have had that have been before thee, neither shall there any after thee have the like.

Figure 6. God gave Solomon more than he asked for

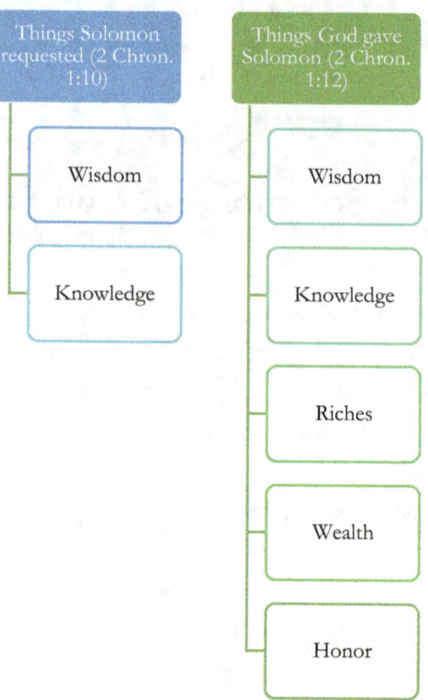

Solomon only asked God for two things, but God was kind to him and gave him five things. The wealth that Solomon obtained was a direct result of God's blessing. More leaders need to have a heart similar to Solomon's and ask for things that relate to the works of God. When persons put God and his works first, he is often willing to bless them with more than what they ask.

James 1:5

⁵ If any of you lack wisdom, let him ask of God, that giveth to all men liberally, and upbraideth not; and it shall be given him.

Wisdom is not something that would be impossible for God to bless people with. Therefore, all believers can ask God for wisdom.

7. Esther put God first

7.1 Mordecai was troubled in his spirit

Mordecai received written information that the king was going to destroy the Jews. He was troubled by this, and he put on sackcloth and mourned. He knew that his life would be in danger, along with the lives of all Jews. He started a one-man protest and prayed. However, Mordecai could not enter the gate because he was not properly clothed. Nevertheless, this did not stop the plan of God from going through, because Mordecai's actions got the attention of Queen Esther. Believers must not be afraid to do what they know is right, since God may send help for them.

Esther 4:1-3

1 When Mordecai perceived all that was done, Mordecai rent his clothes, and put on sackcloth with ashes, and went out into the midst of the city, and cried with a loud and a bitter cry; 2 And came even before the king's gate: for none might enter into the king's gate clothed with sackcloth. 3 And in every province, whithersoever the king's commandment and his decree came, there was great mourning among the Jews, and fasting, and weeping, and wailing; and many lay in sackcloth and ashes.

7.2 Esther was moved by Mordecai's actions and words

Esther's eunuchs and female attendants came to her and told her what happened with her cousin; she and Mordecai were both moved. She decided to send him clothes, but he refused her assistance and continued to wear his sackcloth. Mordecai was troubled about the lives of the people of God who were going to be destroyed because of the king's order, and he wanted something to be done to prevent God's people from being destroyed. Mordecai must be commended for loving the people of God, rather than being selfish and thinking only of himself.

Queen Esther was aware of the law concerning anyone visiting the king before a set time. She did not want to disobey the law, but her cousin was not going to allow the laws of the king to cause the Jewish people to perish. There need to be more persons with the same attitude Mordecai showed in these times, putting the business of God first and then everything else after.

Queen Esther was caught in a tough position: she had to decide if she wanted to please her cousin or please the king. Mordecai's communication to Esther was that if she did not take action, her life would be in danger (Esther 4:12-14). These words from Mordecai troubled Esther, and she was moved to make a decision.

Esther 4:4-8

⁴ So Esther's maids and her chamberlains came and told it her. Then was the queen exceedingly grieved; and she sent raiment to clothe Mordecai, and to take away his sackcloth from him: but he received it not. ⁵ Then called Esther for Hatach, one of the king's chamberlains, whom he had appointed to attend upon her, and gave him a commandment to Mordecai, to know what it was, and why it was. ⁶ So Hatach went forth to Mordecai unto the street of the city, which was before the king's gate. ⁷ And Mordecai told him of all that had happened unto him, and of the sum of the money that Haman had promised to pay to the king's treasuries for the Jews, to destroy them. ⁸ Also he gave him the copy of the writing of the decree that was given at Shushan to destroy them, to shew it unto Esther, and to declare it unto her, and to charge her that she should go in unto the king, to make supplication unto him, and to make request before him for her people.

Thankfully, Esther was not only a queen with beauty, but a queen who knew her God. Esther was willing to put God first.

Figure 7. Esther used her royal office and God to save the Jews

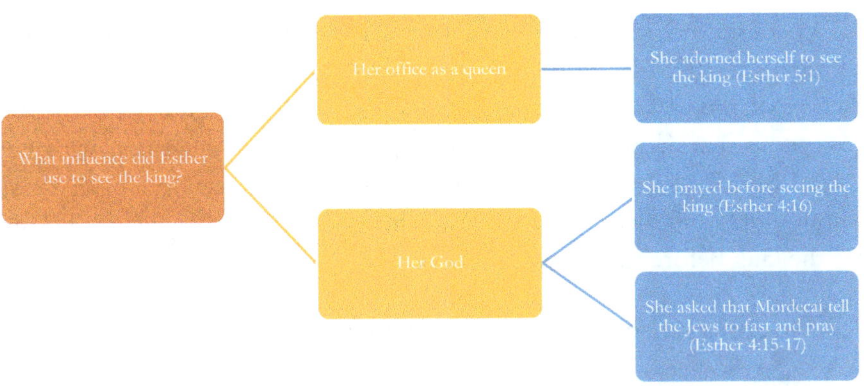

Esther 4:9-17

9 And Hatach came and told Esther the words of Mordecai. 10 Again Esther spake unto Hatach, and gave him commandment unto Mordecai; 11 All the king's servants, and the people of the king's provinces, do know, that whosoever, whether man or women, shall come unto the king into the inner court, who is not called, there is one law of his to put him to death, except such to whom the king shall hold out the golden sceptre, that he may live: but I have not been called to come in unto the king these thirty days. 12 And they told to Mordecai Esther's words. 13 Then Mordecai commanded to answer Esther, Think not with thyself that thou shalt escape in the king's house, more than all the Jews. 14 For if thou altogether holdest thy peace at this time, then shall there enlargement and deliverance arise to the Jews from another place; but thou and thy father's house shall be destroyed: and who knoweth whether thou art come to the kingdom for such a time as this?

15 Then Esther bade them return Mordecai this answer, 16 Go, gather together all the Jews that are present in Shushan, and fast ye for me, and neither eat nor drink three days, night or day: I also and my maidens will fast likewise; and so will I go in unto the king, which is not according to the law: and if I perish, I perish. *¹⁷ So Mordecai went his way, and did according to all that Esther had commanded him.*

Queen Esther knew the law that if she went to see the king before the set time, it could result in her death, but on this occasion, she was willing to die for the things of God (Esther 4:16).

What Queen Esther did was remarkable. She was not prepared to go in her own strength, but she went in the strength of the name of the Lord. She asked that the children of God pray and fast for three days (Esther 4:16). Take note that at no time was Esther in direct communication with her cousin Mordecai, but she relied on the information received from those whom she sent to meet him. She trusted her cousin and was willing to go and see the king before the set time.

7.3 Queen Esther got the king's attention

In the third day of fasting and praying, Queen Esther went to see the king. When the king saw her, he inquired of her request and had the option to refuse to see her, but he was willing to meet with her. When people put God first, their God can make any wicked leader want to see and hear from them, as we see in the life of Queen Esther.

Figure 8. God worked on King Ahasuerus' heart when Esther and the Jews prayed

Esther got to see the king before the set time (Esther 5:1-2)

The king was wiling to listen to her (Esther 5:3)

The king was willing to offer half of his kingdom to Esther (Esther 5:3)

God was already working on Queen Esther's behalf. Take note that before the king even heard Esther's request, he made a generous proposal to grant her request and to give her half of the kingdom (Esther 5:3, 6). When people put God first, God will cause favor to flow upon them, even from persons who planned to do them evil.

Esther 5:1-9

1 Now it came to pass on the third day, that Esther put on her royal apparel, and stood in the inner court of the king's house, over against the king's house: and the king sat upon his royal throne in the royal house, over against the gate of the house. 2 And it was so, when the king saw Esther the queen standing in the court, that she obtained favour in his sight: and the king held out to Esther the golden sceptre that was in his hand. So Esther drew near, and touched the top of the sceptre. 3 Then said the king unto her, What wilt thou, queen Esther? and what is thy request? it shall be even given thee to the half of the kingdom. 4 And Esther answered, If it seem good unto the king, let the king and Haman come this day unto the banquet that I have prepared for him. 5 Then the king said, Cause Haman to make haste, that he may do as Esther hath said. So the king and Haman came to the banquet that Esther had prepared. 6 And the king said unto Esther at the banquet of wine, What is thy petition? and it shall be granted thee: and what is thy request? even to the half of the kingdom it shall be performed. 7 Then answered Esther, and said, My petition and my request is; 8 If I have found favour in the sight of the king, and if it please the king to grant my petition, and to perform my request, let the king and Haman come to the banquet that I shall prepare for them, and I will do to morrow as the king hath said. 9 Then went Haman forth that day joyful and with a glad heart: but when Haman saw Mordecai in the king's gate, that he stood not up, nor moved for him, he was full of indignation against Mordecai.

7.4 King Ahasuerus listened to Mordecai because of Esther

It might have been difficult for Mordecai to get the king's attention concerning the danger that was planned for the Jews. However, Mordecai used his influence through his cousin, a believer, and the king was prepared to sit down and listen to Mordecai.

Esther 6:1-6

1 On that night could not the king sleep, and he commanded to bring the book of records of the chronicles; and they were read before the king. 2 And it was found written, that Mordecai had told of Bigthana and Teresh, two of the king's chamberlains, the keepers of the door, who sought to lay hand on the king Ahasuerus. ³And the king said, What honour and dignity hath been done to Mordecai for this? Then said the king's servants that ministered unto him, There is nothing done for him. ⁴And the king said, Who is in the court? Now Haman was come into the outward court of the king's house, to speak unto the king to hang Mordecai on the gallows that he had prepared for him. ⁵And the king's servants said unto him, Behold, Haman standeth in the court. And the king said, Let him come in. ⁶So Haman came in. And the king said unto him, What shall be done unto the man whom the king delighteth to honour? Now Haman thought in his heart, To whom would the king delight to do honour more than to myself?

7.5 Esther asked that the people of God be saved

Esther was not thinking of her personal glory, but of seeing the Jews saved. So, on the second day of her banquet, King Ahasuerus asked her to state her petition to him. It is not normal for a king to ask a person to state their petition four times (Esther 5:3, 6; 7:3; 9:12). On the third occasion of the king's request, Queen Esther was willing to tell him what she wanted him to do. She was patient as she waited, because she knew that God was working on her behalf.

Esther 7:1-4

¹So the king and Haman came to banquet with Esther the queen. ²And the king said again unto Esther on the second day at the banquet of wine, What is thy petition, queen Esther? and it shall be granted thee: and what is thy request? and it shall be performed, even to the half of the kingdom. ³Then Esther the queen answered and said, If I have found favour in thy sight, O king, and if it please the king, let my life be given me at my petition, and my people at my request: ⁴For we are sold, I and my people, to be destroyed, to be slain, and to perish. But if we had been sold for bondmen and bondwomen, I had held my tongue, although the enemy could not countervail the king's damage.

7.6 Haman was destroyed by his own evil trap

After King Ahasuerus listened to Esther's petition, he was outraged at the person who wanted to hurt the people of Queen Esther. The king was not going to let that happen, so he was willing to protect Esther and her people.

Esther 7:5-10

⁵ Then the king Ahasuerus answered and said unto Esther the queen, Who is he, and where is he, that durst presume in his heart to do so? ⁶ And Esther said, The adversary and enemy is this wicked Haman. Then Haman was afraid before the king and the queen. ⁷ And the king arising from the banquet of wine in his wrath went into the palace garden: and Haman stood up to make request for his life to Esther the queen; for he saw that there was evil determined against him by the king. ⁸ Then the king returned out of the palace garden into the place of the banquet of wine; and Haman was fallen upon the bed whereon Esther was. Then said the king, Will he force the queen also before me in the house? As the word went out of king's mouth, they covered Haman's face. ⁹ And Harbonah, one of the chamberlains, said before the king, Behold also, the gallows fifty cubits high, which Haman had made for Mordecai, who spoken good for the king, standeth in the house of Haman. Then the king said, Hang him thereon. ¹⁰ So they hanged Haman on the gallows that he had prepared for Mordecai. Then was the king's wrath pacified.

Haman thought that it was time to plead for his own life, but it was too late. The trap he had set up against Mordecai was the same trap that would destroy him. When the people of God place their God first in their lives, their God will turn things around in their favor.

7.7 God protected and restored the Jews because of Esther

The life of Haman was taken, but more than that, the king was willing to restore to the Jews that which they had lost. Mordecai got the estate of his enemy, Haman. All this became possible because Queen Esther put God first in her life. Esther was willing to relate to the king that Mordecai was her family (Esther 8:1). She chose not to reveal her family connection to the king before Mordecai had spoken with the king. This was a wise move from Esther, since the king was able to direct the estate of Haman to Mordecai because he was Esther's family.

Esther was not yet done with the king. She knew that if the king were to die, the law would still remain that the Jews were to be destroyed. So she went again to the king and asked him to write a new law, which would give the Jews the rights to settle in the land. The king was willing to grant Queen Esther another request. He went so far as to inform his subjects that whatever Mordecai will request, they will put it into law and the king will sign it (Esther 8:7-10).

Mordecai and Esther were able to have fun days because they put God first in their lives and their God was fighting on their behalf. They got more than they had bargained for, because God had already softened the king's heart as the Jews fasted and prayed.

Esther 8:1-14

1 On that day did the king Ahasuerus give the house of Haman the Jews' enemy unto Esther the queen. And Mordecai came before the king; for Esther had told what he was unto her. 2 And the king took off his ring, which he had taken from Haman, and gave it unto Mordecai. And Esther set Mordecai over the house of Haman. 3 And Esther spake yet again before the king, and fell down at his feet, and besought him with tears to put away the mischief of Haman the Agagite, and his device that he had devised against the Jews. 4 Then the king held out the golden sceptre toward Esther. So Esther arose, and stood before the king, 5 And said, If it please the king, and if I have favour in his sight, and the thing seem right before the king, and I be pleasing in his eyes, let it be written to reverse the letters devised by Haman the son of Hammedatha the Agagite, which he wrote to destroy the Jews which are in all the king's provinces: 6 For how can I endure to see the evil that shall come unto my people? or how can I endure to see the destruction of my kindred? 7 Then the king Ahasuerus said unto Esther the queen and to Mordecai the Jew, Behold, I have given Esther the house of Haman, and him they have hanged upon the gallows, because he laid his hand upon the Jews. 8 Write ye also for the Jews, as it liketh you, in the king's name, and seal it with the king's ring: for the writing which is written in the king's name, and sealed with the king's ring, may no man reverse.

9 Then were the king's scribes called at that time in the third month, that is, the month Sivan, on the three and twentieth day thereof; and it was written according to all that Mordecai commanded unto the Jews, and to the lieutenants, and the deputies and rulers of the provinces which are from India unto Ethiopia, an hundred twenty and seven provinces, unto every province according to the writing thereof, and unto every people after their language, and to the Jews according to their writing, and according to their language. 10 And he wrote in the king Ahasuerus' name, and sealed it with the king's ring, and sent letters by posts on horseback, and riders on mules, camels, and young dromedaries: 11 Wherein the king granted the Jews which were in every city to gather themselves together, and to stand for their life, to destroy, to slay and to cause to perish, all the power of the people and province that would assault them, both little ones and women, and to take the spoil of them for a prey, 12 Upon one day in all the provinces of king

Ahasuerus, namely, upon the thirteenth day of the twelfth month, which is the month Adar. ¹³ The copy of the writing for a commandment to be given in every province was published unto all people, and that the Jews should be ready against that day to avenge themselves on their enemies. ¹⁴ So the posts that rode upon mules and camels went out, being hastened and pressed on by the king's commandment. And the decree was given at Shushan the palace.

7.8 Mordecai went from sackcloth to royal apparel

It was Mordecai's time to rejoice. His burden for God's people did not go in vain, and he proved that his God was fighting on his behalf. Mordecai was now sporting new clothing and looking like royalty.

Figure 9. Mordecai's great accomplishments

Esther 8:1-2	Esther 8:5-10	Esther 8:15	Esther 9:4	Esther 10:2-3
• The estate of Haman was given to Mordecai	• The laws were changed to allow the Jews to settle in the land	• Royal clothes for Mordecai	• He was a powerful man in the king's palace and was feared by many	• He was promoted to be second in charge of the land

Esther 8:15-17

¹⁵ And Mordecai went out from the presence of the king in royal apparel of blue and white, and with a great crown of gold, and with a garment of fine linen and purple: and the city of Shushan rejoiced and was glad. ¹⁶ The Jews had light, and gladness, and joy, and honour. ¹⁷ And in every province, and in every city, whithersoever the king's commandment and his decree came, the Jews had joy and gladness, a feast and a good day. And many of the people of the land became Jews; for the fear of the Jews fell upon them.

7.9 The Jews were in control

It was now the Jews' time to be in control. The Jews were powerful and were supported by the king. Those who had caused harm to the Jews were destroyed by their hand, because God had turned the battle around to give the Jews victory over their enemies. The new law was proclaimed throughout the land, so everyone knew that the Jews were now in control.

Esther 9:1-32

1 Now in the twelfth month, that is, the month Adar, on the thirteenth day of the same, when the king's commandment and his decree drew near to be put in execution, in the day that the enemies of the Jews hoped to have power over them, (though it was turned to the contrary, that the Jews had rule over them that hated them;) 2 The Jews gathered themselves together in their cities throughout all the provinces of the king Ahasuerus, to lay hand on such as sought their hurt: and no man could withstand them; for the fear of them fell upon all people. 3 And all the rulers of the provinces, and the lieutenants, and the deputies, and officers of the king, helped the Jews; because the fear of Mordecai fell upon them. 4 For Mordecai was great in the king's house, and his fame went out throughout all the provinces: for this man Mordecai waxed greater and greater.

5 Thus the Jews smote all their enemies with the stroke of the sword, and slaughter, and destruction, and did what they would unto those that hated them. 6 And in Shushan the palace the Jews slew and destroyed five hundred men. 7 And Parshandatha, and Dalphon, and Aspatha, 8 And Poratha, and Adalia, and Aridatha, 9 And Parmashta, and Arisai, and Aridai, and Vajezatha, 10 The ten sons of Haman the son of Hammedatha, the enemy of the Jews, slew they; but on the spoil laid they not their hand.

11 On that day the number of those that were slain in Shushan the palace was brought before the king. 12 And the king said unto Esther the queen, The Jews have slain and destroyed five hundred men in Shushan the palace, and the ten sons of Haman; what have they done in the rest of the king's provinces? now what is thy petition? and it shall be granted thee: or what is thy request further? and it shall be done. 13 Then said Esther, If it please the king, let it be granted to the Jews which are in Shushan to do to morrow also according unto this day's decree, and let Haman's ten sons be hanged upon the gallows. 14 And the king commanded it so to be done: and the decree was given at Shushan; and they hanged Haman's ten sons.

15 For the Jews that were in Shushan gathered themselves together on the fourteenth day also of the month Adar, and slew three hundred men at Shushan; but on the prey they laid not their hand. 16 But the other Jews that were in the king's provinces gathered themselves together, and stood for their lives, and had rest from their enemies, and slew of their foes seventy and five thousand, but they laid not their hands on the prey, 17 On the thirteenth day of the month Adar; and on the fourteenth day of the same rested they, and made it a day of feasting and gladness. 18 But the Jews that were at Shushan assembled together on the thirteenth day thereof, and on the fourteenth thereof; and on the fifteenth day of the same they rested, and made it a day of feasting and gladness. **19** *Therefore the Jews of the villages, that dwelt in the unwalled towns, made the fourteenth day of the month Adar a day of gladness and feasting, and a good day, and of sending portions one to another.*

20 *And Mordecai wrote these things, and sent letters unto all the Jews that were in all the provinces of the king Ahasuerus, both nigh and far,* **21** *To stablish this among them, that they should keep the fourteenth day of the month Adar, and the fifteenth day of the same, yearly,* **22** *As the days wherein the Jews rested from their enemies, and the month which was turned unto them from sorrow to joy, and from mourning into a good day: that they should make them days of feasting and joy, and of sending portions one to another, and gifts to the poor.* **23** *And the Jews undertook to do as they had begun, and as Mordecai had written unto them;* **24** *Because Haman the son of Hammedatha, the Agagite, the enemy of all the Jews, had devised against the Jews to destroy them, and had cast Pur, that is, the lot, to consume them, and to destroy them;* **25** *But when Esther came before the king, he commanded by letters that his wicked device, which he devised against the Jews, should return upon his own head, and that he and his sons should be hanged on the gallows.*

26 *Wherefore they called these days Purim after the name of Pur. Therefore for all the words of this letter, and of that which they had seen concerning this matter, and which had come unto them,* **27** *The Jews ordained, and took upon them, and upon their seed, and upon all such as joined themselves unto them, so as it should not fail, that they would keep these two days according to their writing, and according to their appointed time every year;* **28** *And that these days should be remembered and kept throughout every generation, every family, every province, and every city; and that these days of Purim should not fail from among the Jews, nor the memorial of them perish from their seed.* **29** *Then Esther the queen, the daughter of Abihail, and Mordecai the Jew, wrote with all authority, to confirm this second letter of Purim.* **30** *And he sent the letters unto all the Jews, to the hundred twenty and seven provinces of the kingdom of Ahasuerus, with words of peace and truth,* **31** *To confirm these days of Purim in their times appointed, according as Mordecai the Jew and Esther the queen had enjoined them, and as they had decreed for themselves and for their seed, the matters of the fastings and their cry.* **32** *And the decree of Esther confirmed these matters of Purim; and it was written in the book.*

7.10 Mordecai's status increased

Mordecai did not only have his victory, but he was promoted. He was the second man in charge, after King Ahasuerus. What a promotion! It all became possible because Mordecai and Queen Esther placed God first in their lives. They were not looking for fame and wealth, but for the protection of God's people, and God was on their side fighting for them.

Esther 10:1-3

1 And the king Ahasuerus laid a tribute upon the land, and upon the isles of the sea. 2 And all the acts of his power and of his might, and the declaration of the greatness of Mordecai, whereunto the king advanced him, are they not written in the book of the chronicles of the kings of Media and Persia? 3 For Mordecai the Jew was next unto king Ahasuerus, and great among the Jews, and accepted of the multitude of his brethren, seeking the wealth of his people, and speaking peace to all his seed.

8. Job put God first

The life of Job was filled with calamity after calamity, yet he put God first. Many other humans would have given up when they experienced the first calamity, but Job was willing to stay with God.

Job's wife provided him with a proposal, and he could have been like some husbands and worked with that proposal, since she saw what he was going through. His wife knew that he loved the Lord and wanted to do everything that God expected him to do. However, she saw that although Job was maintaining his faith with God, he was experiencing life-threatening difficulties.

The suffering that Job was going through appeared to be unbearable, but Job did not plan to quit on his God. His faith in God was unmoved by external things, because Job was expecting God to deliver him sometime soon.

Job 2:1-13

¹Again there was a day when the sons of God came to present themselves before the LORD, and Satan came also among them to present himself before the LORD. ²And the LORD said unto Satan, From whence comest thou? And Satan answered the LORD, and said, From going to and fro in the earth, and from walking up and down in it. ³And the LORD said unto Satan, Hast thou considered my servant Job, that there is none like him in the earth, a perfect and an upright man, one that feareth God, and escheweth evil? and still he holdeth fast his integrity, although thou movedst me against him, to destroy him without cause. ⁴And Satan answered the LORD, and said, Skin for skin, yea, all that a man hath will he give for his life. ⁵But put forth thine hand now, and touch his bone and his flesh, and he will curse thee to thy face. ⁶And the LORD said unto Satan, Behold, he is in thine hand; but save his life.

⁷So went Satan forth from the presence of the LORD, and smote Job with sore boils from the sole of his foot unto his crown. ⁸And he took him a potsherd to scrape himself withal; and he sat down among the ashes. ⁹Then said his wife unto him, Dost thou still retain thine integrity? curse God, and die. 10 But he said unto her, Thou speakest as one of the foolish women speaketh. What? shall we receive good at the hand of God, and shall we not receive evil? In all this did not Job sin with his lips.

11 Now when Job's three friends heard of all this evil that was come upon him, they came every one from his own place; Eliphaz the Temanite, and Bildad the Shuhite, and Zophar the Naamathite: for they had made an appointment together to come to mourn with him and to comfort him. 12 And when they lifted up their eyes afar off, and knew him not, they lifted up their voice, and wept; and they rent every one his mantle, and sprinkled dust upon their heads toward heaven. 13 So they sat down with him upon the ground seven days and seven nights, and none spake a word unto him: for they saw that his grief was very great.

While God had great blessings in store for Job, there were three major calamities that happened to him on day two. His wife told him that he had an option to curse God, but Job did not take that option. It is often seen that when an individual is going through one calamity, another one suddenly strikes them before they can recover. Job experienced this problem, but he did not lose faith in God. Just imagine three major calamities striking Job in one day.

Figure 10. Job's calamities on day two

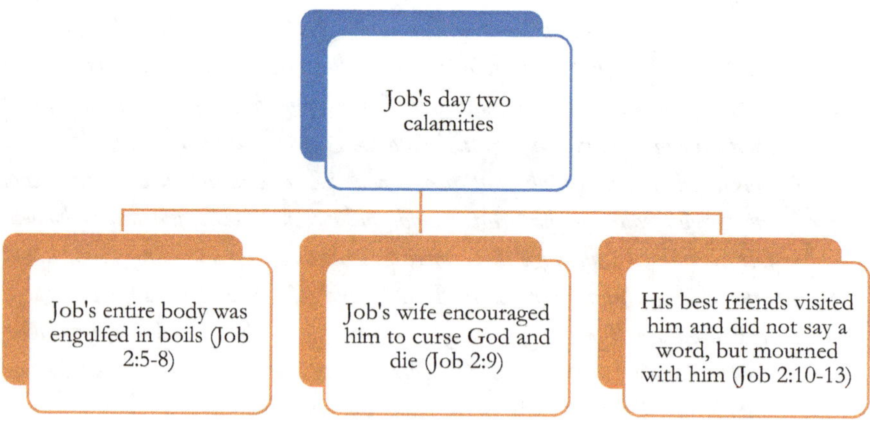

Job chose to answer his wife in a non-confrontational manner and did not allow his calamities to determine his response. He kept his cool, because he wanted God to get the glory from his calamities.

Job 13:15

15 Though he slay me, yet will I trust in him: but I will maintain mine own ways before him.

Ephesians 4:26

26 Be ye angry, and sin not: let not the sun go down upon your wrath.

8.1 God blessed Job for his faithfulness

After all Job went through, and after God proved that Job was faithful to him, it was God who honored his words and blessed Job. Indeed, the Lord was delighted to give his son what he deserved. If Job had not put God first during his calamities, then he would not have received God's blessings, as can be seen in Job 42:1-16.

Job 42:10-17

10 And the LORD turned the captivity of Job, when he prayed for his friends: also the LORD gave Job twice as much as he had before. 11 Then came there unto him all his brethren, and all his sisters, and all they that had been of his acquaintance before, and did eat bread with him in his house: and they bemoaned him, and comforted him over all the evil that the LORD had brought upon him: every man also gave him a piece of money, and every one an earring of gold. 12 So the LORD blessed the latter end of Job more than his beginning: for he had fourteen thousand sheep, and six thousand camels, and a thousand yoke of oxen, and a thousand she asses. 13 He had also seven sons and three daughters. 14 And he called the name of the first, Jemima; and the name of the second, Kezia; and the name of the third, Kerenhappuch. 15 And in all the land were no women found so fair as the daughters of Job: and their father gave them inheritance among their brethren. 16 After this lived Job an hundred and forty years, and saw his sons, and his sons' sons, even four generations. 17 So Job died, being old and full of days.

God gave Job double portions of blessings, so Job now received from God more than he had anticipated. God is always looking to bless those who put him first in every situation.

9. Daniel put God first

Daniel, one of the major prophets, served at a time when the king had passed a decree that if anyone was found bowing down to their gods, there would be harsh penalty against them. The other leaders who served the king went to him and complained that Daniel was not following the king's decree. The reports from the other leaders made the king angry.

However, Daniel knew his God and was not troubled with the decisions and actions that the king might take. When a person knows their God, they must not be fearful of what earthly leaders will do, because they know that their God will deliver them. It can be a tough decision, but God likes to prove himself in tough situations.

In Daniel 6:1-9, we read that other leaders did not want Daniel to be a leader to serve the king. However, Daniel put God first and prayed to his God (Daniel 6:10-11). It must be noted that Daniel could have closed the window when he went to pray, but he kept the window open, because he knew that his God would deliver him.

The king was furious over Daniel's decision and threw him in the lion's den (Daniel 6:10-18). Because Daniel had placed his God first, the lion did not do anything to Daniel, which is a very strange thing. Because Daniel allowed God to be foremost in his life, God shut the lion's mouth.

Daniel 6:1-22

¹ It pleased Darius to set over the kingdom an hundred and twenty princes, which should be over the whole kingdom; ² And over these three presidents; of whom Daniel was first: that the princes might give accounts unto them, and the king should have no damage. ³ Then this Daniel was preferred above the presidents and princes, because an excellent spirit was in him; and the king thought to set him over the whole realm. ⁴ Then the presidents and princes sought to find occasion against Daniel concerning the kingdom; but they could find none occasion nor fault; forasmuch as he was faithful, neither was there any error or fault found in him. ⁵Then said these men, We shall not find any occasion against this Daniel, except we find it against him concerning the law of his God.

⁶Then these presidents and princes assembled together to the king, and said thus unto him, King Darius, live for ever. ⁷All the presidents of the kingdom, the governors, and the princes, the counsellors, and the captains, have consulted together to establish a royal statute, and to make a firm decree, that whosoever shall ask a petition of any God or man for thirty days, save of thee, O king, he shall be cast into the den of lions. ⁸Now, O king, establish the decree, and sign the writing, that it be not changed, according to the law of the Medes and Persians, which altereth not. ⁹Wherefore king Darius signed the writing and the decree.

¹⁰Now when Daniel knew that the writing was signed, he went into his house; and his windows being open in his chamber toward Jerusalem, he kneeled upon his knees three times a day, and prayed, and gave thanks before his God, as he did aforetime. ¹¹Then these men assembled, and found Daniel praying and making supplication before his

¹²Then they came near, and spake before the king concerning the king's decree; Hast thou not signed a decree, that every man that shall ask a petition of any God or man within thirty days, save of thee, O king, shall be cast into the den of lions? The king answered and said, The thing is true, according to the law of the Medes and Persians, which altereth not. ¹³Then answered they and said before the king, That Daniel, who is of the children of the captivity of Judah, regardeth not thee, O king, nor the decree that thou hast signed, but maketh his petition three times a day. ¹⁴Then the king, when he heard these words, was sore displeased with himself, and set his heart on Daniel to deliver him: and he laboured till the going down of the sun to deliver him.

¹⁵Then these men assembled unto the king, and said unto the king, Know, O king, that the law of the Medes and Persians is, That no decree nor statute which the king establisheth may be changed. ¹⁶Then the king commanded, and they brought Daniel, and cast him into the den of lions. Now the king spake and said unto Daniel, Thy God whom thou servest continually, he will deliver thee. ¹⁷And a stone was brought and laid upon the mouth of the den; and the king sealed it with his own signet, and with the signet of his lords; that the purpose might not be changed concerning Daniel. ¹⁸Then the king went to his palace and passed the night fasting: neither were instruments of musick brought before him: and his sleep went from him.

¹⁹Then the king arose very early in the morning and went in haste unto the den of lions. ²⁰And when he came to the den, he cried with a lamentable voice unto

Daniel: and the king spake and said to Daniel, O Daniel, servant of the living God, is thy God, whom thou servest continually, able to deliver thee from the lions? 21 Then said Daniel unto the king, O king, live for ever. 22 My God hath sent his angel, and hath shut the lions' mouths, that they have not hurt me: forasmuch as before him innocency was found in me; and also, before thee, O king, have I done no hurt.

9.1 God restored Daniel

After the king looked and saw that Daniel was alive, he knew that it had to be the God of Daniel that preserved his life while he was among the lions. The same king that ordered for Daniel to be thrown into the lion's den was now willing to promote Daniel. King Darius even spoke about the power and protection of Daniel's God. All this became possible because Daniel did not bow down to the king's decree, but stood up for his God.

Daniel 6:23-27

23 Then was the king exceedingly glad for him and commanded that they should take Daniel up out of the den. So Daniel was taken up out of the den, and no manner of hurt was found upon him, because he believed in his God. 24 And the king commanded, and they brought those men which had accused Daniel, and they cast them into the den of lions, them, their children, and their wives; and the lions had the mastery of them, and brake all their bones in pieces or ever they came at the bottom of the den. 25 Then king Darius wrote unto all people, nations, and languages, that dwell in all the earth; Peace be multiplied unto you. 26 I make a decree, That in every dominion of my kingdom men tremble and fear before the God of Daniel: for he is the living God, and stedfast for ever, and his kingdom that which shall not be destroyed, and his dominion shall be even unto the end. 27 He delivereth and rescueth, and he worketh signs and wonders in heaven and in earth, who hath delivered Daniel from the power of the lions.

The psalmist was able to talk about God's ability to restore his children who walk upright. Believers must be confident that if God has called them and sent them on an assignment, he will be there for them.

Psalm 84:11

11 For the LORD God is a sun and shield: the LORD will give grace and glory: no good thing will he withhold from them that walk uprightly.

10. Shadrach, Meshach, and Abednego put God first

Very often when a leader gives an order, they expect the order to be followed. However, these three servants of God were not willing to follow King Nebuchadnezzar's order but only to follow the true and living God. Because these three servants refused to follow the king's instruction, their lives were in danger. What is important is that these three servants put God first and did not want to compromise their integrity with the Lord. They preferred to refuse the king's request, which was a violation of God's requirement for his children.

Since these three men refused the king's order, the king ordered that the furnace be heated seven times hotter, as he wanted to put an end to those who refused his order. The heat was so great that it could consume these three men as soon as they were thrown into it. However, because these men put God first, the heat from the furnace did not affect them.

Daniel 3:12-23

12 There are certain Jews whom thou hast set over the affairs of the province of Babylon, Shadrach, Meshach, and Abednego; these men, O king, have not regarded thee: they serve not thy gods, nor worship the golden image which thou hast set up. 13 Then Nebuchadnezzar in his rage and fury commanded to bring Shadrach, Meshach, and Abednego. Then they brought these men before the king. 14 Nebuchadnezzar spake and said unto them, Is it true, O Shadrach, Meshach, and Abednego, do not ye serve my gods, nor worship the golden image which I have set up? 15 Now if ye be ready that at what time ye hear the sound of the cornet, flute, harp, sackbut, psaltery, and dulcimer, and all kinds of musick, ye fall down and worship the image which I have made; well: but if ye worship not, ye shall be cast the same hour into the midst of a burning fiery furnace; and who is that God that shall deliver you out of my hands?

16 Shadrach, Meshach, and Abednego, answered and said to the king, O Nebuchadnezzar, we are not careful to answer thee in this matter. 17 If it be so, our God whom we serve is able to deliver us from the burning fiery furnace, and he will deliver us out of thine hand, O king. 18 But if not, be it known unto thee, O king, that we will not serve thy gods, nor worship the golden image which thou hast set up.

19 Then was Nebuchadnezzar full of fury, and the form of his visage was changed against Shadrach, Meshach, and Abednego: therefore he spake, and commanded that they should heat the furnace one seven times more than it was wont to be heated. 20 And he commanded the most mighty men that were in his army to bind Shadrach, Meshach, and Abednego, and to cast them into the burning fiery furnace. 21 Then these men were bound in their coats, their hosen, and their hats, and their other garments, and were cast into the midst of the burning fiery furnace. 22 Therefore because the king's commandment was urgent, and the furnace exceeding hot, the flames of the fire slew those men that took up Shadrach, Meshach, and Abednego. 23 And these three men, Shadrach, Meshach, and Abednego, fell down bound into the midst of the burning fiery furnace.

10.1 God protected his sons

After the king ordered that these three men be thrown in the furnace, he expected them to die. However, there was a strange occurrence that marveled the king.

Daniel 3:24-25

24 Then Nebuchadnezzar the king was astonished, and rose up in haste, and spake, and said unto his counsellors, Did not we cast three men bound into the midst of the fire? They answered and said unto the king, True, O king. 25 He answered and said, Lo, I see four men loose, walking in the midst of the fire, and they have no hurt; and the form of the fourth is like the Son of God.

Figure 11. Strange appearances in the furnace

Three men were thrown in the furnace, but four men were there (Dan. 3:24)

The fourth person had an appearance like the Son of God (Dan. 3:25)

The men had been bound, then thrown in the furnace, but they were walking (Dan. 3:25)

10.2 Nebuchadnezzar was astonished

King Nebuchadnezzar was astonished by what God had done for these men. The king knew that he threw three men in the fire, but when he looked into the furnace, he saw another person with them. The king said that the fourth person in the fire appeared to be the Son of God. Take note that even a king who planned to do evil could recognize the presence of God.

These three men were taken out of the furnace alive and in good health. Those who put God first will see God fighting on their behalf.

Daniel 3:26-30

26 Then Nebuchadnezzar came near to the mouth of the burning fiery furnace, and spake, and said, Shadrach, Meshach, and Abednego, ye servants of the most high God, come forth, and come hither. Then Shadrach, Meshach, and Abednego, came forth of the midst of the fire. 27 And the princes, governors, and captains, and the king's counsellors, being gathered together, saw these men, upon whose bodies the fire had no power, nor was an hair of their head singed, neither were their coats changed, nor the smell of fire had passed on them. 28 Then Nebuchadnezzar spake, and said, Blessed be the God of Shadrach, Meshach, and Abednego, who hath sent his angel, and delivered his servants that trusted in him, and have changed the king's word, and yielded their bodies, that they might not serve nor worship any god, except their own God. 29 Therefore I make a decree, That every people, nation, and language, which speak any thing amiss against the God of Shadrach, Meshach, and Abednego, shall be cut in pieces, and their houses shall be made a dunghill: because there is no other God that can deliver after this sort. 30 Then the king promoted Shadrach, Meshach, and Abednego, in the province of Babylon.

11. A few loaves of bread and fishes fed a multitude

During his ministry, Jesus performed many miracles, and there were many persons who followed him for the miracles. Jesus wanted to make sure that the lives of persons were better.

His teaching ministry was also well known. People followed him because they wanted to get fresh knowledge. As he was teaching one day, a great multitude of people gathered to listen to him. Jesus had a great following without the use of social media or the mainstream media to promote his works.

When Jesus saw the great multitude that followed him on this day and sat down to listen to him, he knew that they would be hungry, and that it was time to feed them. This is a caring act from a leader who has a heart for people's social needs.

The disciples and Jesus did not have any food with them. However, Jesus did not panic, because he knew that if he put his Father first, then all other matters would be taken care of.

John 6:1-15

1 After these things Jesus went over the sea of Galilee, which is the sea of Tiberias. 2 And a great multitude followed him, because they saw his miracles which he did on them that were diseased. 3 And Jesus went up into a mountain, and there he sat with his disciples. 4 And the passover, a feast of the Jews, was nigh. 5 When Jesus then lifted up his eyes, and saw a great company come unto him, he saith unto Philip, Whence shall we buy bread, that these may eat? 6 And this he said to prove him: for he himself knew what he would do. 7 Philip answered him, Two hundred pennyworth of bread is not sufficient for them, that every one of them may take a little. 8 One of his disciples, Andrew, Simon Peter's brother, saith unto him, 9 There is a lad here, which hath five barley loaves, and two small fishes: but what are they among so many?

10 And Jesus said, Make the men sit down. Now there was much grass in the place. So the men sat down, in number about five thousand. 11 And Jesus took the loaves; and when he had given thanks, he distributed to the disciples, and the disciples to them that were set down; and likewise of the fishes as much as they would. 12 When they were filled, he said unto his disciples, Gather up the fragments that remain, that nothing be lost. 13 Therefore they gathered them together, and filled twelve baskets with the fragments of the five barley loaves, which remained over and above unto them that had eaten. 14 Then those men, when they had seen the miracle that Jesus did, said, This is of a truth that prophet that should come into the world. 15 When Jesus therefore perceived that they would come and take him by force, to make him a king, he departed again into a mountain himself alone.

What is interesting about this passage of scripture is that Jesus knew that the bread and fishes were not enough to feed the people. Nevertheless, Jesus put God first and blessed the bread and fishes, then asked the disciples to share them among the people. After the people finished eating, Jesus asked his disciples to collect what remained. This was another miracle that Jesus performed, as the amount of bread that remained was even greater than the amount distributed. Because Jesus placed God first in this situation, God came through for him: all the people were fed, and the remainder was greater than the amount shared with the people.

12. Paul and Silas put God first

Saul was called by Jesus on the Damascus road as he was on his way to persecute the believers. The call of Jesus on the life of anyone will cause them to have great success, but they will also experience many challenges. Apostle Paul, whose name was changed from Saul, had to endure many challenges as he worked for the Lord.

Apostle Paul went to many missions for the Lord, and he took other believers with him. On this occasion according to Acts 16, he and Silas were going to the house of the Lord to pray. As they continued their journey to the house of the Lord, they passed through the village, and a young lady who was involved in fortune-telling recognized that they had the Spirit of God on them. Paul and Silas did not give much attention to her and the evil works that she was doing, but she continued to follow them for days and said that they were servants of God (Acts 16:17-18). Paul looked at her and cast out the evil spirit from her, and that was when their problems started.

Acts 16:16-40

16 And it came to pass, as we went to prayer, a certain damsel possessed with a spirit of divination met us, which brought her masters much gain by soothsaying: 17 The same followed Paul and us, and cried, saying, These men are the servants of the most high God, which shew unto us the way of salvation. 18 And this did she many days. But Paul, being grieved, turned and said to the spirit, I command thee in the name of Jesus Christ to come out of her. And he came out the same hour.

19 And when her masters saw that the hope of their gains was gone, they caught Paul and Silas, and drew them into the marketplace unto the rulers, 20 And brought them to the magistrates, saying, These men, being Jews, do exceedingly trouble our city, 21 And teach customs, which are not lawful for us to receive, neither to observe, being Romans. 22 And the multitude rose up together against them: and the magistrates rent off their clothes, and commanded to beat them. 23 And when they had laid many stripes upon them, they cast them into prison, charging the jailor to keep them safely: 24 Who, having received such a charge, thrust them into the inner prison, and made their feet fast in the stocks.

25 And at midnight Paul and Silas prayed, and sang praises unto God: and the prisoners heard them. 26 And suddenly there was a great earthquake, so that the foundations of the prison were shaken: and immediately all the doors were opened, and every one's bands were loosed. 27 And the keeper of the prison awaking out of his sleep, and seeing the prison doors open, he drew out his sword, and would have killed himself, supposing that the prisoners had been fled. 28 But Paul cried with a loud voice, saying, Do thyself no harm: for we are all here. 29 Then he called for a light, and sprang in, and came trembling, and fell down before Paul and Silas, 30 And brought them out, and said, Sirs, what must I do to be saved? 31 And they said, Believe on the Lord Jesus Christ, and thou shalt be saved, and thy house.

32 And they spake unto him the word of the Lord, and to all that were in his house. 33 And he took them the same hour of the night, and washed their stripes; and was baptized, he and all his, straightway. 34 And when he had brought them into his house, he set meat before them, and rejoiced, believing in God with all his house. 35 And when it was day, the magistrates sent the serjeants, saying, Let those men go. 36 And the keeper of the prison told this saying to Paul, The magistrates have sent to let you go: now therefore depart, and go in peace. 37 But Paul said unto them, They have beaten us openly uncondemned, being Romans, and have cast us into prison; and now do they thrust us out privily? nay verily; but let them come themselves and fetch us out. 38 And the serjeants told these words unto the magistrates: and they feared, when they heard that they were Romans. 39 And they came and besought them, and brought them out, and desired them to depart out of the city. 40 And they went out of the prison, and entered into the house of Lydia: and when they had seen the brethren, they comforted them, and departed.

12.1 Paul and Silas endured bad treatment while working for God

These servants of God were treated with inhumane behavior, yet they followed God without murmuring. They continued to put God first during their prison experience, and God came through for them (Acts 16:23-33). No one likes to be in prison, but what is very interesting is that these men were sent to prison for working for the Lord. When believers go through difficult situations as they work for God, they sometimes want to quit, but Paul and Silas prayed and praised God while they were in prison (Acts 16:25-26).

Figure 12. Bad treatment against Paul and Silas for doing God's work

12.2 God got the victory

Many persons would feel that what these servants of God went through was an embarrassment, but God got the victory during their trials. These men put God first in their lives, and God was able to shake the foundation of the prison and set them free.

Figure 13. Good things that happened through Paul and Silas' wrongful imprisonment

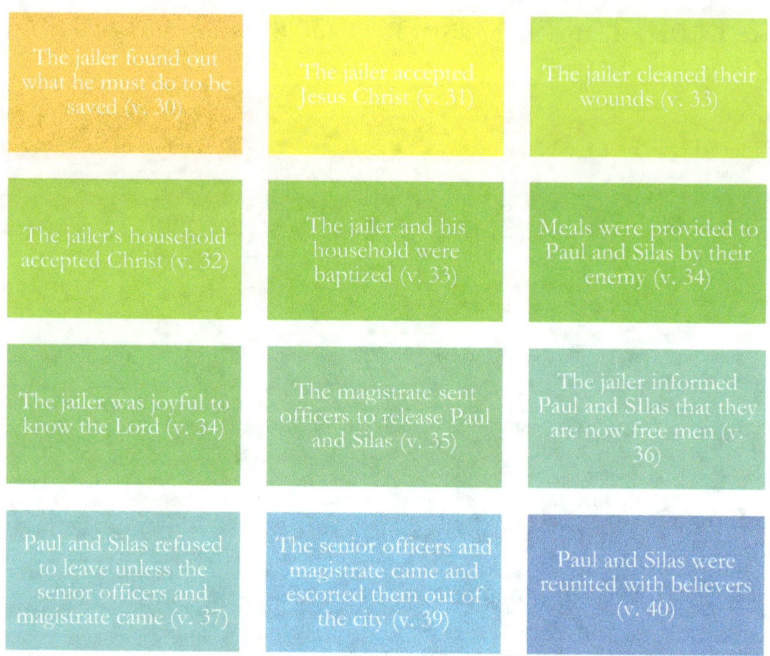

If you are going through a difficult situation while serving the Lord, do not stop serving God. Continue to put God first in your life and in every situation, and your God will give you the victory. When God causes you to overcome, he will save many souls. God may only be using you as a vessel to get his victory.

About the Author

Since giving his life to the Lord in 1986, Geary Reid has experienced many challenges. However, he knows that the Christian journey will always have challenges. In his early stage of serving the Lord, he tried to do many things in his own strength, and he failed. As he spent much time learning about the Lord, he recognized that if God is placed first in his life, then he will have many victories.

Rev. Reid has placed God first in his life ever since, and he has seen what the Lord has done whenever he is placed first in the lives of believers. Therefore, Rev. Reid is advocating for more believers to move from trusting themselves to placing their trust in God in order to make their lives better. He knows that there are times when some situations may look very difficult, but when God is given the opportunity to reign in the lives of believers, great things will happen for them.

While author Geary Reid is a full-time employee at his workplace, he sees the need to place God first in many situations. He knows that some situations can be overwhelming, but he has seen the hands of God give him the victory.

Reid knows that he is never completely familiar with God, so in every situation, he has to trust God. While many situations may appear to be similar, there is always the need to depend upon God, since Satan is an experienced deceiver and will come as an angel of light.

As Rev. Reid teaches believers, he constantly reminds them to search the scriptures for persons who overcame their challenges. He tells persons that his own life is not the best example, so they must use the Bible as their guide.

No believer can overcome Satan with their own strength; however, if they place God first in their lives, then they will have victory, similar to that which Reid has experienced.

Every day when Reid drives to work, he places God first over his journey. He knows that even the best driver can be caught in an accident, even when they are doing the right thing. However, with the protection of God, Reid is able to travel daily and return home safely to his family. Even when he goes to preach at different churches, he still seeks God's direction and wisdom, since he has learned not to depend upon his own wisdom.

The Bible remains important literature for all believers to be acquainted with. As they search God's Word, they will see how many persons were able to overcome their challenges. Reid continues to search the scriptures as his source of inspiration for standing strong in the Lord.

This page is intentionally left blank

This page is intentionally left blank

This page is intentionally left blank

This page is intentionally left blank

This page is intentionally left blank

This page is intentionally left blank

This page is intentionally left blank

This page is intentionally left blank

This page is intentionally left blank

This page is intentionally left blank

This page is intentionally left blank